The Sacred Col...

Low Voice

MW00668942

Compiled and Edited by Richard Walters

ISBN 0-634-03073-6

HAL•LEONARD®
CORPORATION

7777 W. BLUEMOUND RD. P.O. BOX 13819 MILWAUKEE, WI 53213

For all works contained herein:
Unauthorized copying, arranging, adapting, recording or public performance is an infringement of copyright.
Infringers are liable under the law.

Visit Hal Leonard Online at
www.halleonard.com

Contents

Concert Arrangements of
Hymns & Sacred Folksongs   arranged by Richard Walters

Contents

Alphabetically by Title

Agnus Dei
(Lamb of God)

Georges Bizet

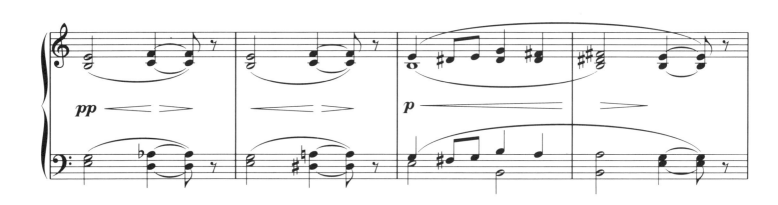

Copyright © 1992 by HAL LEONARD CORPORATION
International Copyright Secured   All Rights Reserved

Ave Maria

César Franck
(1822 - 1890)

Copyright © 2001 by HAL LEONARD CORPORATION
International Copyright Secured   All Rights Reserved

Ave Maria

Franz Schubert

Copyright © 1992 by HAL LEONARD CORPORATION
International Copyright Secured   All Rights Reserved

A - ve Ma - ri -
A - ve Ma - ri -

a!
a!

dim.

Ave Maria
(adapted from "Prelude in C" by J.S. Bach)

Charles Gounod

Copyright © 1992 by HAL LEONARD CORPORATION
International Copyright Secured   All Rights Reserved

19

Be Near Me Still

Prayer

English version by
Alma Strettell

Ferdinand Hiller, Op. 46

Moderato

Herr! den ich tief im Her- zen tra- ge, sei du mit
Lord! in my heart's love deep I hide Thee, Be near me

mir, du Gna- den- hort in Glück und Pla- ge, sei du mit
still! Thou tow'r of strength, what- e'er be- tide me, Be Thou with

mir. Be- hü- te mich am Born der Freu- de vor Ü- ber- muth, und
me. Oh be my guard in life's bright plac- es, Lest pride pre- vail, When

Copyright © 2001 by HAL LEONARD CORPORATION
International Copyright Secured   All Rights Reserved

wenn ich an mir selbst ver - za - ge, sei du mit mir.
fear or self - mis - trust o'er - ride me, *Be near me still!*

Dein Se - gen ist wie Thau den Re - ben, nichts kann ich
Like dew up - on the vine Thy grace is, *I'm not a -*

selbst, doch dass ich kühn das Höch - ste wa - ge, sei du mit
lone, *But when I storm the heights, then guide me To do Thy*

mir, sei du mit mir. O du mein Trost,
will; *Be near me still!* *O Thou my hope,*

du mei - ne Stär - ke, mein Son - nen - licht, _____
my pow'r un - shak - en, My soul's true sun, _____

bis an das En - de mei - ner Ta - ge, sei du mit
Till earth's dark days shall be for - sak - en, Be near me

mir, sei du mit mir, bis an das En - de mei - ner
still! be near me still! Till earth's dark days shall be for -

Ta - ge, sei du mit mir, mit mir. _____
sak - en, Be near me, near me still! _____

Clouds and Darkness

Antonín Dvořák, Op. 99

Copyright © 2001 by HAL LEONARD CORPORATION
International Copyright Secured   All Rights Reserved

ta - tion.   From His pres - ence

go - eth fire and con - sum - eth all _____ His

Poco più mosso

en - e-mies.   For   His   light - nings have

light - en'd   the   world,   the   earth   be - held   and

Meno maestoso

trem - bled.   Moun - tains shall melt as wax   at   His

pres - ence,   when the   Might - y One   com - eth   to   judg - ment.   The

poco rit.

heav - ens de-clare His truth and   right - eous-ness,   and all the earth re - joic - eth   in   His

great - ness.

a tempo

f *più mosso*   *ff*   *rit.*   *pp*

Lord, Thou Art My Refuge

Antonín Dvořák

Lord, Thou art my ref - uge and _____ my shield, and

in Thy word put I my trust.

Out of my sight,

Copyright © 2001 by HAL LEONARD CORPORATION
International Copyright Secured   All Rights Reserved

ye that do e - vil, for my heart is fixed,

I will hold fast to God's com-mand - ments.

Streng-then me, that I may keep ___ Thy law,

and that Thy stat - utes may be my ___ de - light.

Hear My Prayer

Antonín Dvořák

Hear my ____ prayer, O Lord, my ____ God!

Oh, hide ____ not Thy

Copyright © 2001 by HAL LEONARD CORPORATION
International Copyright Secured   All Rights Reserved

face from my pe - ti - tion.

Bow thine ear to me and

heark - en un - to the voice of my mourn - ing,

to the voice of my mourn - ing.

Pain - ed sore is my

heart with-in, and trem - bling hath fal - len up-

on me, the fear of death o - ver -

Meno

whelms me. Hear my sigh - ing!

Un poco più mosso

Oh,

had I but ea - gle's pin - ions,

had I wings like the sil - ver

dove! Far a - way ____ would I wan - der, I would hide me in the wil - der - ness. On wings I would has - ten to hide from the storm, the storm __ and fear - ful tem - pest.

God Is My Shepherd

Antonín Dvořák

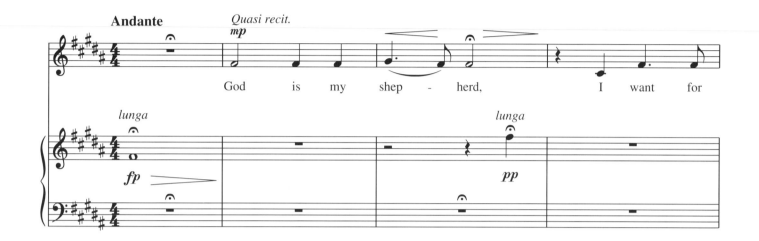

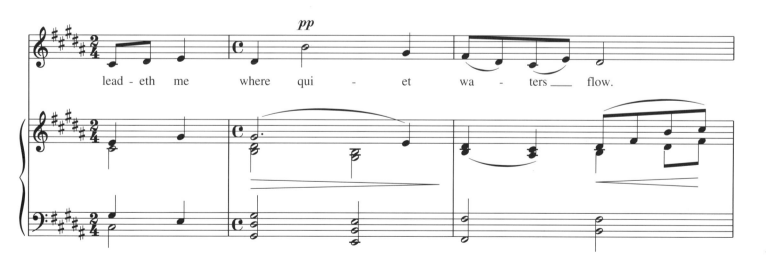

Copyright © 2001 by HAL LEONARD CORPORATION
International Copyright Secured   All Rights Reserved

My faint - ing soul doth
He re - store and guid - eth me in the ways of peace, to
glo - ri - fy His name. And
though in death's dark val - ley my steps must

wan - der, my spir - it shall ___ not fear, for

Thou art by me _____ still.

molto rit.

a tempo

Thy _____ rod and staff are with me, and they shall ___ com - fort

me.

I Will Sing New Songs

Antonín Dvořák

Copyright © 2001 by HAL LEONARD CORPORATION
International Copyright Secured   All Rights Reserved

By the Waters of Babylon

Antonín Dvořák

Copyright © 2001 by HAL LEONARD CORPORATION
International Copyright Secured   All Rights Reserved

mem - ber'd thee, O Zi - on.

As for our harps, we

hang - ed them up on the wil - low trees. For

accel.

they that had brought us to mis - e - ry

accel.

asked of us a joy - ful song. Yea, they did

speak to us with mock - ing words:

"Sing us now, sing us one of the

songs _____ of Zi - on!"

Hear My Prayer, O Lord

Antonín Dvořák

Copyright © 2001 by HAL LEONARD CORPORATION
International Copyright Secured   All Rights Reserved

I will dwell ___ for - ev - er in Thy tents ___ and hide me in the shad - ow of Thy wings.

Lord! ___

Thou art in - deed my God, yea, I will seek Thee

ear - ly. My soul is faint, my bod - y long - eth,

long - eth af - ter Thee

in a bar - ren de - sert where there is no wa - ter.

53

Turn Thee to Me

Antonín Dvořák

Copyright © 2001 by HAL LEONARD CORPORATION
International Copyright Secured   All Rights Reserved

great are the sor - rows of my — heart; bring me out of my ————— dis -

tress, bring me out of my ————— dis -

tress. Oh be mer - ci - ful,

look on my sor - row, see mine af - flic - tion and for - give me all my

wick - ed - ness. Oh, keep my soul in safe - ty and de -

liv - er me. Let me nev - er be con - found - ed

for my hope is in Thee,

for my hope is in Thee, ___ in Thee.

I Will Lift Mine Eyes

Antonín Dvořák

Andante con moto

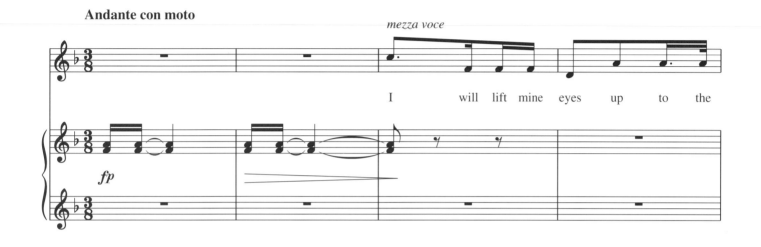

I will lift mine eyes up to the

moun-tains whence _ com - eth my

help.

Copyright © 2001 by HAL LEONARD CORPORATION
International Copyright Secured   All Rights Reserved

Sing Ye a Joyful Song

Antonín Dvořák

Allegro moderato

mezza voce

Sing ye a joy - ful song

un - to the Lord, ___ Who hath done mar - vel - ous,

Copyright © 2001 by HAL LEONARD CORPORATION
International Copyright Secured   All Rights Reserved

mar - vel - ous things.

Praise the Lord all the earth! Sing prais - es, shout and be

joy - ful.

Moun - tains, clap your hands for joy.

Let the fields laugh and sing with wav - ing

corn, and let _____ all the trees _____ of the for -

rit. *a tempo*

- est be joy - ful!

rit. *ff* *f*

a tempo

Dank sei Dir, Herr
(Thanks Be to God)

Siegfried Ochs*
(Previously attributed to Handel)

*Siegfried Ochs (1858-1929) claimed to have discovered an aria by Handel, and to have made an arrangement of the piece, which was published and became well-known. Closer research has revealed that this is actually an original composition by Ochs.

Copyright © 1992 by HAL LEONARD CORPORATION
International Copyright Secured All Rights Reserved

ra - el   hin   durch   das   Meer.
grate - ful   thanks   be   to   Thee.

con espressione

sempre f

sempre f

pp

Wie ei - ne___ Her - de zog___ es hin - durch,_____
Like a___ great___ flock Thy hand___ ev - er led___ us,

p

p

Herr,_____ Dei - ne Hand schütz - te es,
Lord,_____ Thy_____ hand leads_____ us,

in Dei - ner___ Gü - te___ gabst Du ihm Heil.
By all___ Thy___ good - ness te___ Sal - va - tion is ours.

mf

Dank _____
Thanks _____

_____ sei Dir, { Dank _____ } sei Dir,
_____ be to God, { opt. { Herr, / Dank _____ } be to

Herr,   Du hast   Dein Volk   mit Dir ge - führt,
God,   Thou who   has made   Thy peo - ple free,

Is -   ra - el hin durch das Meer.
All -   grate - ful thanks be to Thee.   *con espressione*

Bist du bei mir

(You Are with Me)

Gottfried Heinrich Stölzel
(Previously attributed to J.S. Bach)

Anonymous

Bist du bei mir, geh' ich mit Freu - den zum Ster - ben und zu mei - ner Ruh', zum Ster - ben und zu mei - ner Ruh'.

You are with me, my joy for - ev - er. Un - til my death and un - to my rest, un - til my death and un - to rest.

Copyright © 1992 by HAL LEONARD CORPORATION
International Copyright Secured   All Rights Reserved

Bist du ___ bei ___ mir, geh' ich mit
You are ___ with ___ me, my joy for -

Freu - den zum Ster - ben ___ und zu mei - ner ___
ev - er. Un - til ___ my ___ death and un - to my

Ruh', zum ___ Ster - ben und zu mei - ner Ruh'.
rest, un - til ___ death and un - to rest.

Ach, wie ver - gnügt wär' so mein
Oh how con - tent all of my

Crucifixus

Jean-Baptiste Faure

Copyright © 1992 by HAL LEONARD CORPORATION
International Copyright Secured   All Rights Reserved

Entreat Me Not to Leave Thee

(Song of Ruth)

From the Book of Ruth 1:16-17

Charles Gounod

Copyright © 1992 by HAL LEONARD CORPORATION
International Copyright Secured   All Rights Reserved

God, _____ my God; _____ Thy

peo - ple shall be my peo - ple, and thy

God, my God. Where thou

di - est, will I die, _____ and there will I be

bur - ied;___ The Lord do so to me, and more al - so, if aught but

death part thee and me, if aught but death ___ part thee and

me. ___ Thy peo - ple shall be my

peo - ple, and thy ___ God, my

God;_____ Thy peo - ple shall be my

peo - ple, and thy God,_____ my

God;_____ Thy peo - ple shall be my

cresc.

f

peo - ple, and thy God,_____ thy

God,   my   God.

Evening Hymn

Words by Dr. William Fuller
Music by Henry Purcell
Realization by Richard Walters

Copyright © 2001 by HAL LEONARD CORPORATION
International Copyright Secured   All Rights Reserved

rest, _____ O ____ my ____ soul! And ____ sing -

- ing praise the mer - cy, that _____ pro - longs thy

days, and sing - ing praise the mer - cy, that ____

____ pro - longs thy days.

Evening Prayer

from *Hansel and Gretel*

Engelbert Humperdinck

Copyright © 2001 by HAL LEONARD CORPORATION
International Copyright Secured   All Rights Reserved

He That Keepeth Israel

Adolphe Schlösser

Copyright © 2001 by HAL LEONARD CORPORATION
International Copyright Secured   All Rights Reserved

slum - bers not, nor sleeps. _____ He will give his

An - gels charge o - ver thee, To keep thee in

all thy ways, _____ in all thy ways, He that

keep - eth Is - ra - el, _____ He that

The Holy City

F. E. Weatherly and Stephen Adams

Andante moderato

Last night I lay a-sleep-ing   There came a dream so fair.   I
then me-thought my dream   was changed, the streets no long - er rang.

stood in old Je - ru - sa - lem, Be - side the tem - ple there;   I
Hushed were the glad Ho - san - nas   The lit - tle child - ren sang;   The

heard the child - ren sing - ing,   And ev - er as they sang,   Me -
sun grew dark with mys - ter - y,   The morn was cold and chill   As the

Copyright © 1992 by HAL LEONARD CORPORATION
International Copyright Secured   All Rights Reserved

Lift up your gates and sing,
Hark how the an - gels sing,
Ho -
san - na in the high - est, Ho -
san - na to your King!
And

And once a-gain the scene was changed, New earth there seemed to __ be, I

saw the Ho - ly Ci - ty Be - side the tide - less sea; The

light of God was on its streets, The gates were o - pen wide, And

all who would might en - ter, And

Jesu, Joy of Man's Desiring

Johann Sebastian Bach
arranged by John Reed

Copyright © 1995 by HAL LEONARD CORPORATION
International Copyright Secured   All Rights Reserved

Love ___ most ___ bright,
mu - sic ___ rings!

Drawn by Thee, our souls as - pir - ing
Where the flock, in Thee con - fid - ing,

Soar to un - cre - a - ted ___
Drink of joy from death - less ___

light.
springs.

Word of God, our flesh _____ that fash - ion'd
Theirs is beau - ty's fair - est plea - sure,

With the fire of
Theirs is wis - dom's

throne.
known.

O Divine Redeemer
(Repentir)

Charles Gounod

Copyright © 1992 by HAL LEONARD CORPORATION
International Copyright Secured   All Rights Reserved

bles - se! / sins! _____ Par- / For-

don - ne! / give me, O / O, di - vin Ré - demp / di - vine Re-

teur! _____ par - donne à ma ___ fai- / deem - er! I pray Thee, grant ___ me ___

bles - se, ___ par - don - ne, par - donne à ma fai- / par - don, ___ and re - mem - ber not, re - mem - ber not, O

tour - ne les coups, mon Sau - veur! O di - vin Ré - demp-
Death shield Thou me, O my God! O, di - vine Re -

teur! _____ par - don - ne
deem - er, have mer - cy!

à ma fai - bles - se!
Help me, my Sav - ior!

Just a Closer Walk with Thee

Traditional American Song
arranged by Richard Walters

Moderately slow gospel style, with a swing beat

I am weak but Thou art strong, ___
Through this world of toil and snares, ___

Je - sus, keep me from all wrong. ___
if I fal - ter, Lord, who cares? ___

Copyright © 2001 by HAL LEONARD CORPORATION
International Copyright Secured   All Rights Reserved

The Palms
(Les Rameaux)

Jean-Baptiste Faure

O'er all the way, green palms and
Sur nos che-mins les ra - meaux

blos - soms gay   Are strewn this day in fes - tal
et les gay fleurs.   Sont ré - pan-dus dans ce grand

Copyright © 1992 by HAL LEONARD CORPORATION
International Copyright Secured   All Rights Reserved

ac - cla - ma - tion. Ho - san - na!
voix ____ ré - pon - de. Ho - san - na!

cresc.

f

ff

Praised ye the Lord! Bless Him who com-eth to bring us sal -
Gloi - re au Sei-gneur! Bé - ni ce - lui qui vient sau-ver le

va - tion.
mon - de!

ff

His word goes forth, and peo - ples by its might
Il a par - lé, les peu - ples à sa voix
Sing and re - joice, O blest Je - ru - sa - lem,
Ré - jou - is - toi, Sain - te Jé - ru - sa - lem,

Once more re - gain free-dom from de - gra - da - tion,
Ont re - cou - vré leur li - ber - té per - du - e,
Of all Thy sons sing the e - man - ci - pa - tion.
De tes en - fants chan - te la dé - li - vran - ce;

Hu - man - i - ty doth give to each his right,
L'hu - ma - ni - té don - ne à cha - cun ses droits,
Through bound - less love the Christ of Beth - le - hem
Par cha - ri - té le Dieu de Beth - lé - em

(rit. last time)

Bless Him who com-eth to bring us sal - va - tion!
Bé - ni ce - lui qui vient sau - ver le mon - de!

*Optional high notes are for the final verse.

Panis Angelicus

César Franck

Copyright © 1992 by HAL LEONARD CORPORATION
International Copyright Secured   All Rights Reserved

There Is a Green Hill Far Away

Charles Gounod

Andante moderato

There is a green hill far a-way, With-
out a cit-y-wall, Where the dear Lord was cru-ci-fied, Who

Copyright © 2001 by HAL LEONARD CORPORATION
International Copyright Secured   All Rights Reserved

136

Saved by His pre - cious blood. There was no oth - er good e - nough To pay the price of sin, He on - ly could un - lock the gate Of Heav'n and let us in. O

dear - ly, dear - ly has He loved. _____

And we must love Him, too, And trust _____ in His re -

deem - ing blood, And trust _____ in His re -

cresc. molto

p

deem - ing blood, And try His works to do, and

dim.

p

Balm in Gilead

Jeremiah 8 : 22

African-American Spiritual
arranged by Harry T. Burleigh

Copyright © 2001 by HAL LEONARD CORPORATION
International Copyright Secured   All Rights Reserved

rit. *a tempo* *mf* *cresc.*

heal the sin - sick soul. Some - times I feel dis -

cour - aged, And think my work's in vain, But

poco rit.

then the Ho - ly Spir - it, Re - vives my soul a -

a tempo

gain ____ There __ is a Balm in Gil - e - ad, to

By An' By

African-American Spiritual
arranged by Harry T. Burleigh

Copyright © 2001 by HAL LEONARD CORPORATION
International Copyright Secured   All Rights Reserved

Deep River

African-American Spiritual
arranged by Harry T. Burleigh

Copyright © 2001 by HAL LEONARD CORPORATION
International Copyright Secured   All Rights Reserved

Couldn't Hear Nobody Pray

African-American Spiritual
arranged by Harry T. Burleigh

Copyright © 2001 by HAL LEONARD CORPORATION
International Copyright Secured   All Rights Reserved

could-n't hear no-bod — y pray, O 'way down yon-der

rit.   *a tempo*

by __ my — self   I could-n't hear no-bod — y pray. { Chil - ly wa - ters! / Hal - le - lu - jah!

rit.   *p*   *a tempo*

could-n't hear no-bod — y pray. { In the Jor - dan! / Trou - bles o - ver!   could-n't hear no-bod — y

p   *p*

pray. { Cross - in' o - ver! / In the king - dom!   could-n't hear no-bod — y pray. { In - to Ca - naan! / With my Je - sus!

Didn't My Lord Deliver Daniel

story from
the Book of Daniel
chapter 6

African-American Spiritual
original arrangement by
Harry T. Burleigh
adapted by Richard Walters

Copyright © 2001 by HAL LEONARD CORPORATION
International Copyright Secured   All Rights Reserved

wind blow west, it blow like the judge - ment _ day, and ev - 'ry poor soul _ that

nev - er did pray _ will be glad to pray _ that day. Did - n't my Lord de - liv - er

Dan - iel, _ de - liv - er Dan - iel, _ de - liv - er Dan - iel? _ Did - n't my Lord de - liv - er

Dan - iel, _____ and why not ev - er - y man? I set my foot on the

Don't You Weep When I'm Gone

Jeremiah 22:10

African-American Spiritual
arranged by Harry T. Burleigh

Copyright © 2001 by HAL LEONARD CORPORATION
International Copyright Secured   All Rights Reserved

He's Just the Same Today

Exodus 14 : 22
1 Samuel 17 : 49

African-American Spiritual
arranged by Harry T. Burleigh

Copyright © 2001 by HAL LEONARD CORPORATION
International Copyright Secured   All Rights Reserved

Jus' _____ the _____ same to-day; An' the God that ___ liv'd in

Mo - ses ___ time, is jus' the same ___ to - day.

When

Da - vid an' ___ Go - li - ah met ___ the wrong a - gainst ___ the

Go Down, Moses
(Let My People Go!)

Exodus 8

African-American Spiritual
arranged by Harry T. Burleigh

When Is - rael was in E - gypt's lan'

Let my peo - ple go, Op - press'd so hard they

could not stan', Let my peo - ple go.

Copyright © 2001 by HAL LEONARD CORPORATION
International Copyright Secured   All Rights Reserved

Go down, Moses, 'Way down in

E - gypt's ___ lan', ___ Tell ___ ole

Pha - roah, to let my peo - ple go.

Thus saith the Lord, bold Mo - ses said, Let my peo - ple go, If not I'll smite your first born dead, Let my peo - ple

Go, Tell It on the Mountain

African-American Spiritual
arranged by Harry T. Burleigh

While

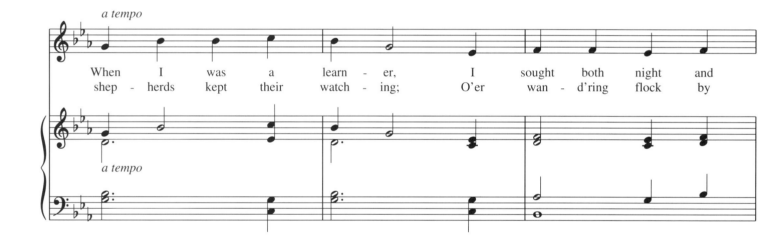

When I was a learn - er, I sought both night and
shep - herds kept their watch - ing; O'er wan - d'ring flock by

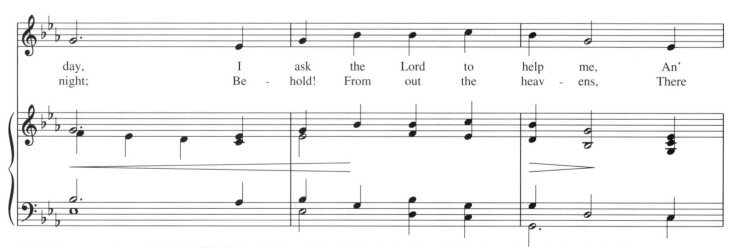

day, I ask the Lord to help me, An'
night; Be - hold! From out the heav - ens, There

Burleigh's arrangement was originally titled "Go Tell It on De Mountains." The singular form "mountain" has become the standard version for this song.

Copyright © 2001 by HAL LEONARD CORPORATION
International Copyright Secured   All Rights Reserved

rall.   *a tempo*

He show me the way. _____ } Go tell it on the
shone a ho - ly light. _____

moun - tain; O - ver the hills an' ev - 'ry - where:

rall.

Go tell it on the moun - tain, Our Je - sus Christ _ is

a tempo

born.

The Gospel Train

African-American Spiritual
arranged by Harry T. Burleigh

Copyright © 2001 by HAL LEONARD CORPORATION
International Copyright Secured   All Rights Reserved

177

I Don't Feel No-Ways Tired

Hebrews 11:14, 16

African-American Spiritual
arranged by Harry T. Burleigh

Moderato

Copyright © 2001 by HAL LEONARD CORPORATION
International Copyright Secured   All Rights Reserved

glo - ry Hal - le - lu - jah!

There's a bet - ter day __ a - com - in' Hal - le - lu -

jah There's a bet - ter day __ a - com - in' Hal - le - lu. _____ When I

leave this worl' __ of __ sor - row, Hal - le - lu - jah For to

I Stood on the River of Jordan

African-American Spiritual
arranged by Harry T. Burleigh

Andante cantabile

I stood on the riv-er of

Jor - dan, To see that ship come sail - in' o - ver,

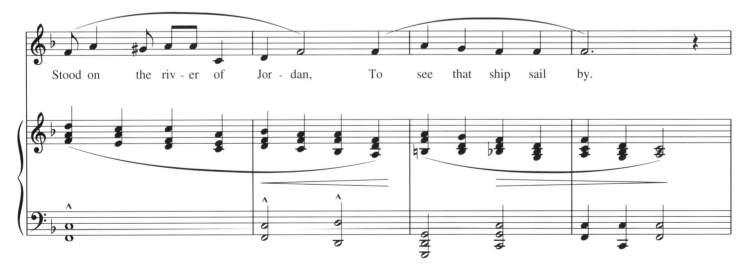

Stood on the riv-er of Jor - dan, To see that ship sail by.

Copyright © 2001 by HAL LEONARD CORPORATION
International Copyright Secured   All Rights Reserved

Oh, mour - ner don't you weep! When you see that ship come

sail - in' o - ver, Oh, mour - ner don't you weep! When you

rit.

see that ship sail by. O

a tempo

sis - ter
broth-er } yo' bet - ter be read - y, To see that ship come sail - in' o - ver,

Sis - ter
Broth-er } you bet - ter be read - y, To see that ship sail by.

Oh, mour-ner don't you weep, When you see that ship come sail - in' o - ver,

Shout Glo - ry Hal - le - lu - jah! When you see that ship sail

by. I stood on the riv - er of Jor - dan!

I Want to Be Ready

Revelation 21 : 16
Acts 2

African-American Spiritual
arranged by Harry T. Burleigh

Copyright © 2001 by HAL LEONARD CORPORATION
International Copyright Secured   All Rights Reserved

Let Us Cheer the Weary Traveler

African-American Spiritual
arranged by Harry T. Burleigh

Copyright © 2001 by HAL LEONARD CORPORATION
International Copyright Secured   All Rights Reserved

191

Little David, Play on Your Harp

African-American Spiritual
arranged by Harry T. Burleigh

Copyright © 2001 by HAL LEONARD CORPORATION
International Copyright Secured   All Rights Reserved

f (quasi recitando) slower

God told Mo - ses, O Lord! Go down in - to E - gypt,

f slower   *decresc.*

O Lord! Tell ole Pha - raoh, O Lord!

a tempo

Loose my peo - ple, O Lit - tle Da - vid; play on your

a tempo

harp, Hal - le - lu, _____ Lit - tle Da - vid,

My Lord, What a Mornin'

text based on
the Book of Revelation, 8 : 10

African-American Spiritual
arranged by Harry T. Burleigh

Copyright © 2001 by HAL LEONARD CORPORATION
International Copyright Secured   All Rights Reserved

Nobody Knows the Trouble I've Seen

African-American Spiritual
arranged by Harry T. Burleigh

Copyright © 2001 by HAL LEONARD CORPORATION
International Copyright Secured   All Rights Reserved

My Way's Cloudy

African-American Spiritual
arranged by Harry T. Burleigh

Oh! breth-er-en, My _____ way, my way's cloud-y,

my _____ way, Go send them an-gels down, Oh! breth-er-en-a,

my _____ way, my way's cloud-y my _____ way, Go

Copyright © 2001 by HAL LEONARD CORPORATION
International Copyright Secured   All Rights Reserved

send them an - gels down Oh! breth - er - en - a, my _____ way,

p   *cresc.*

my way's cloud - y my _____ way, Go

rit.   *a tempo*

send them an - gels down. Ole Sa - tan's mad an' I am glad,

rit.

f *a tempo*

Send them an - gels down, He miss'd the soul he thought he had, O

O Rocks, Don't Fall on Me

African-American Spiritual
arranged by Harry T. Burleigh

Copyright © 2001 by HAL LEONARD CORPORATION
International Copyright Secured   All Rights Reserved

Oh, Didn't It Rain

Genesis 7 : 4

African-American Spiritual
arranged by Harry T. Burleigh

Copyright © 2001 by HAL LEONARD CORPORATION
International Copyright Secured   All Rights Reserved

Sinner, Please Don't Let
This Harvest Pass

African-American Spiritual
arranged by Harry T. Burleigh

Copyright © 2001 by HAL LEONARD CORPORATION
International Copyright Secured   All Rights Reserved

Sometimes I Feel Like a Motherless Child

African-American Spiritual
arranged by Harry T. Burleigh

Copyright © 2001 by HAL LEONARD CORPORATION
International Copyright Secured   All Rights Reserved

'Tis Me, O Lord

African-American Spiritual
arranged by Harry T. Burleigh

Copyright © 2001 by HAL LEONARD CORPORATION
International Copyright Secured   All Rights Reserved

Steal Away

African-American Spiritual
arranged by Harry T. Burleigh

Adagio e molto espressivo

Copyright © 2001 by HAL LEONARD CORPORATION
International Copyright Secured   All Rights Reserved

trum-pet sounds with-in-a my soul; I ain' got long to stay here.

Steal a-way, steal a-way, steal a-way to

Je - sus! Steal a-way; steal ___ a-way home, I

ain' got long to stay here! Green trees are bend-ing, Poor

Swing Low, Sweet Chariot

African-American Spiritual
arranged by Harry T. Burleigh

Copyright © 2001 by HAL LEONARD CORPORATION
International Copyright Secured   All Rights Reserved

Wade in the Water

African-American Spiritual
arranged by Harry T. Burleigh

Copyright © 2001 by HAL LEONARD CORPORATION
International Copyright Secured   All Rights Reserved

a tempo

wa - ter See that band all dress'd in white, ___ God's a - goin' to troub - le the wa - ter. The Lead - er ___ looks like the Is - rael - ite, ___ God's a - goin' to troub - le the wa - ter.

Wade ___ in the wa - ter, Wade ___ in the

Weepin' Mary

John 20 : 11

African-American Spiritual
arranged by Harry T. Burleigh

Copyright © 2001 by HAL LEONARD CORPORATION
International Copyright Secured   All Rights Reserved

an - y -bod - y here like weep - in' _____ Ma - ry, Call up - on your

Je - sus, an' He'll draw nigh O, _____ glo - ry,

glo - ry hal - le - lu - jah! Glo - ry be to my God, who

rules on high! _____

You May Bury Me in the East

1 Corinthians 15 : 52

African-American Spiritual
arranged by Harry T. Burleigh

Copyright © 2001 by HAL LEONARD CORPORATION
International Copyright Secured   All Rights Reserved

for Steve

Be Thou My Vision

Ancient Irish
translated by Mary E. Byrne, 1905
versified by Eleanor H. Hull, 1912

Traditional Irish Melody
arranged by Richard Walters

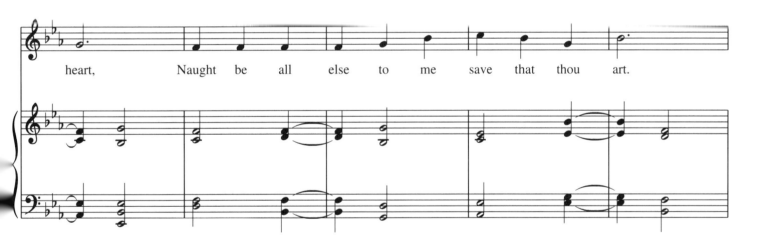

Copyright © 1993 by HAL LEONARD CORPORATION
International Copyright Secured   All Rights Reserved

on - ly, first in my heart, _____

High King of heav - en, my ___ trea - sure thou art. _____

mp espressivo

(8)

High King of heav - en, my vic - tor - y won,

opt.

f

May I reach heav'n's joys, O bright heav-en's sun!

Heart of ____ my ____ own heart, what - ev - er be - fall, ____

Still be my vi - sion, O ru - ler of all. ____

* From here to the end maybe either *piano* or *forte,* depending on the singer's best attributes.

for Sharon
Ah, Holy Jesus

Johann Heermann, 1630
translated by Robert S. Bridges, 1899

"Herzliebster Jesu"
Johann Crüger, 1640
arranged by Richard Walters

Steady, expressive

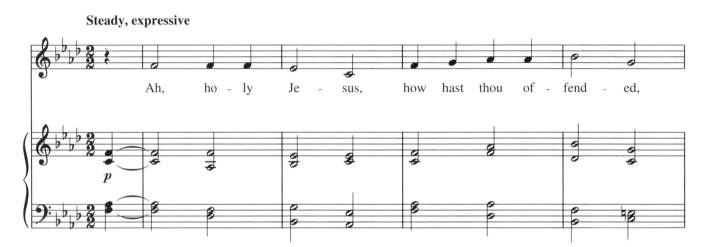

Ah, ho - ly Je - sus, how hast thou of - fend - ed,

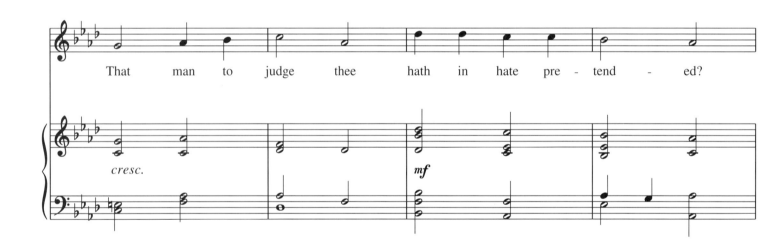

That man to judge thee hath in hate pre - tend - ed?

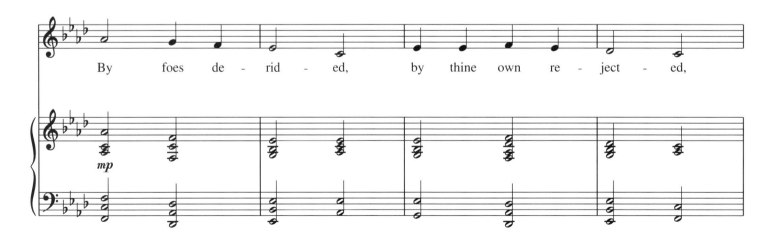

By foes de - rid - ed, by thine own re - ject - ed,

Copyright © 1993 by HAL LEONARD CORPORATION
International Copyright Secured   All Rights Reserved

O most af - flict - ed! Who was the

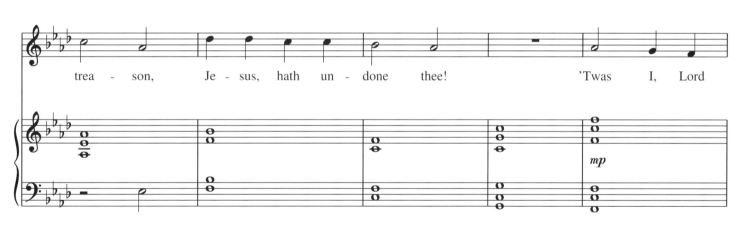

guil - ty? Who brought this up - on thee? A - las, my

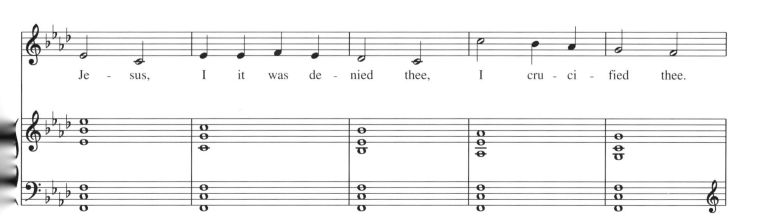

trea - son, Je - sus, hath un - done thee! 'Twas I, Lord

Je - sus, I it was de - nied thee, I cru - ci - fied thee.

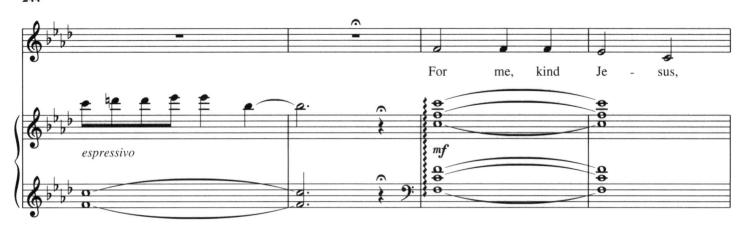

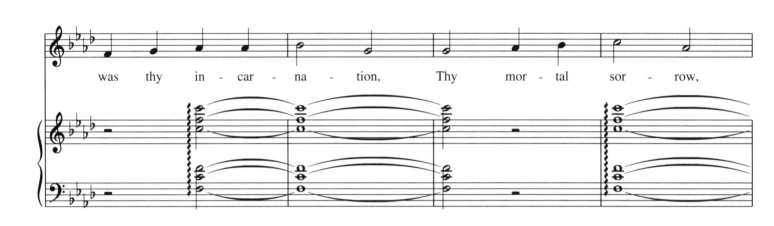

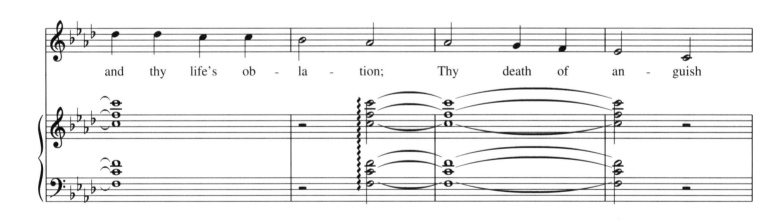

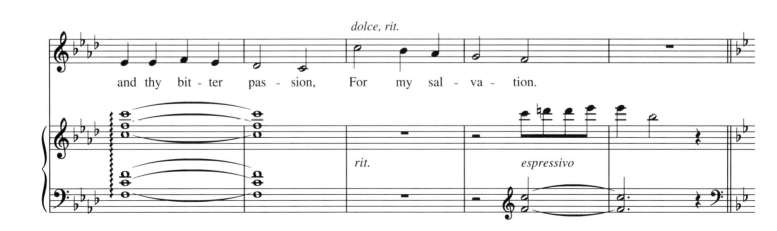

for Carol and Anne

All Creatures of Our God and King

after Psalm 148
Francis of Assisi, c. 1225
translated by William Draper (alt.)

"Lasst uns Erfreuen"
melody from
Geistliche Kirchengesäng, Cologne 1623
adapted by Ralph Vaughan Williams, 1906
arranged by Richard Walters

Copyright © 1993 by HAL LEONARD CORPORATION
International Copyright Secured   All Rights Reserved

burn-ing sun with gold-en beam, _____ Thou sil-ver moon with soft-er

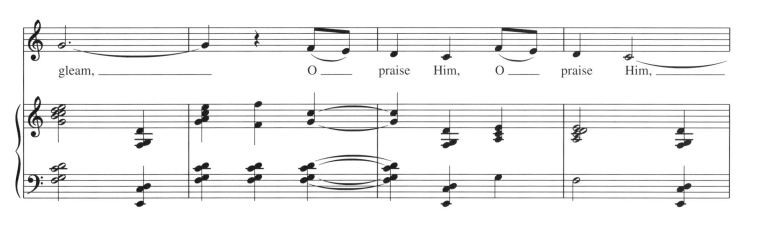

gleam, _____ O ____ praise Him, O ____ praise Him, _____

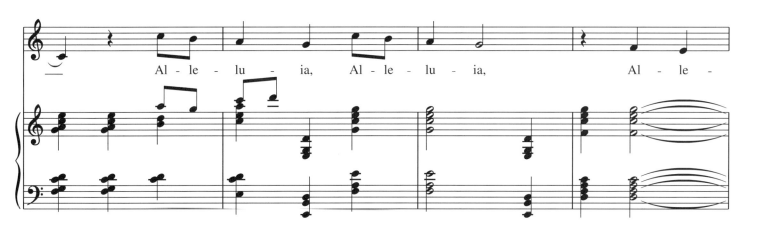

___ Al - le - lu - ia, Al - le - lu - ia, Al - le -

Allegretto **High voice:**

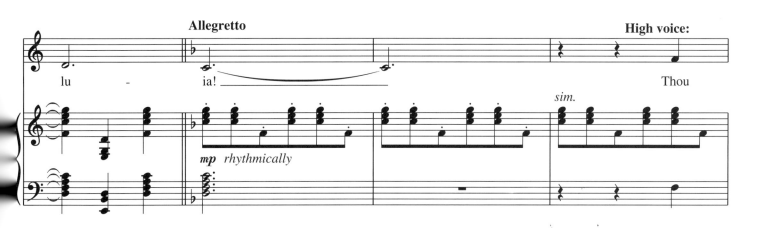

lu - ia! _____ Thou

mp rhythmically

rush-ing wind that are so strong,_____ Ye clouds that sail in heav'n a -

long,_____ O __ praise Him, Al - le - lu - ia! _____

____ Thou ris - ing morn, in praise re - joice, _____ Ye

lights of eve-ning, find a voice, _____ O __ praise Him, O __

praise Him, _____ Al - le - lu - ia, Al - le -

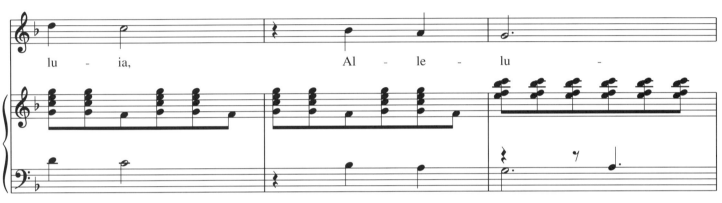

lu - ia, Al - le - lu -

ia! _____

Thou flow-ing wa-ter, pure and clear, _____ Make

Thou flow-ing wa-ter, pure and clear, _____

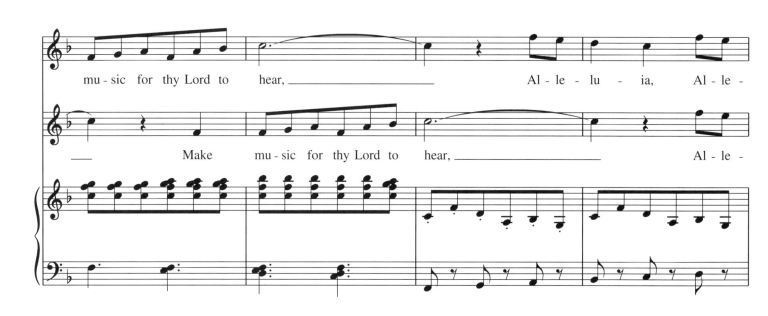

mu-sic for thy Lord to hear, _____ Al-le-lu-ia, Al-le-

Make mu-sic for thy Lord to hear, _____ Al-le-

lu-ia! _____ Thou fire so mas-ter-ful and bright, That

lu-ia, Al-le-lu-ia! _____ Thou fire so mas-ter-ful and

giv - est man both warmth and light,＿＿＿＿＿＿＿＿＿ O＿ praise Him,＿＿＿＿＿

bright, That giv - est man both warmth and light, O＿

＿ Al - le - lu - ia,＿＿＿＿＿＿＿＿ Al - le - lu -

praise Him,＿＿＿＿＿＿＿＿ Al - le - lu - ia, Al - le - lu -

ia!＿＿＿＿＿＿＿＿＿＿＿＿

ia!＿＿＿＿＿＿＿＿＿＿＿＿

accelerando poco a poco ‐ ‐ ‐ ‐ ‐ ‐ ‐ ‐ ‐ ‐ ‐ ‐ ‐ ‐ ‐ ‐

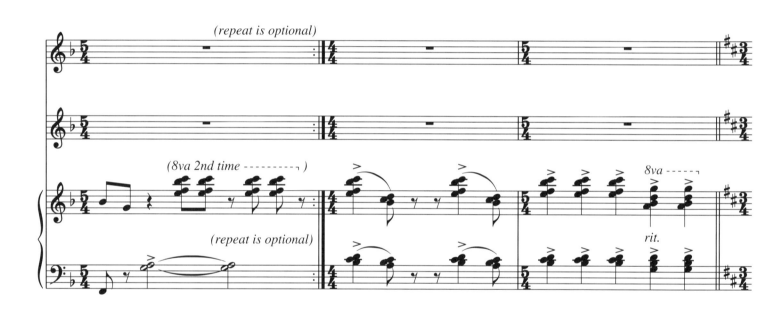

flow, Praise Him, all crea-tures here be - low;

wor - ship him in hum - ble - ness, O ____ praise Him, Al - le -

8vb

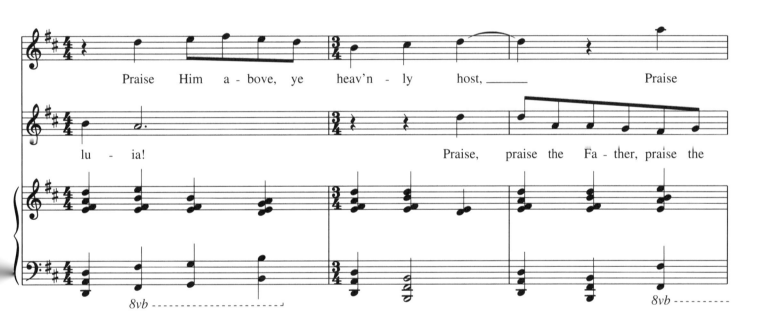

Praise Him a - bove, ye heav'n - ly host, ____ Praise

lu - ia! Praise, praise the Fa - ther, praise the

8vb   *8vb*

Fa - ther, Son and Ho - ly Ghost. ____

Son, And praise the Spi - rit, Three in One. ____

(8)

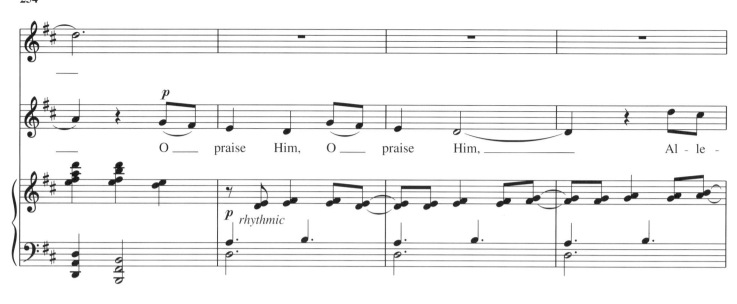

for Kimm

Come, Thou Fount
of Every Blessing

Robert Robinson, 1758

American Folk Tune
First set by John Wyeth, 1813
arranged by Richard Walters

Copyright © 1993 by HAL LEONARD CORPORATION
International Copyright Secured   All Rights Reserved

for Carol and Anne

How Can I Keep from Singing

American Folksong
Arranged by Richard Walters

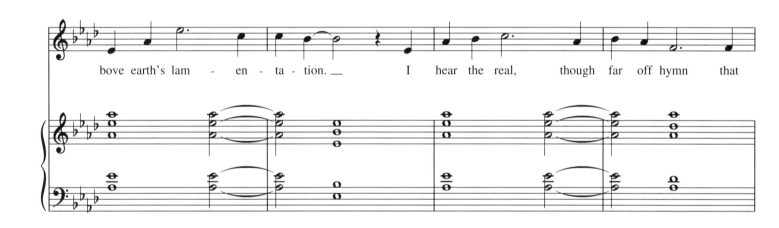

Copyright © 2001 by HAL LEONARD CORPORATION
International Copyright Secured   All Rights Reserved

to that rock I'm cling - ing. __ It sounds an ech - o __ in my soul. How

High Voice

mf

can I keep from sing - ing? __ What though the tem - pest round me rears, I

mp leggiero

know the truth, it liv - eth. __ What though the dark - ness round me close, Songs

in the night it giv - eth. __ No storm can shake my in - most calm while

8va- -

for Russ and Rose Marie

How Firm a Foundation

John Rippon's *A Selection of Hymns,* 1787

Early American Melody
arranged by Richard Walters

Copyright © 1993 by HAL LEONARD CORPORATION
International Copyright Secured   All Rights Reserved

ex - cel - lent word! What more can he say than to

you he hath said, To ___ you who for ref - uge to

Je - sus have fled?

ni - po - tent hand.

mf

p cresc. *mf* *decresc.*

p

When ___

mp

through the deep wa - ters I call thee to go, The ___

p

soul that on Je - sus hath leaned for re - pose I ___

for Robert

Let Us Break Bread Together

African–American Spiritual
arranged by Richard Walters

Steady

Let us break bread to-geth-er on our knees, _____ Let us break bread to-geth-er on our knees. _____ When I fall on my knees, with my

Copyright © 1993 by HAL LEONARD CORPORATION
International Copyright Secured   All Rights Reserved

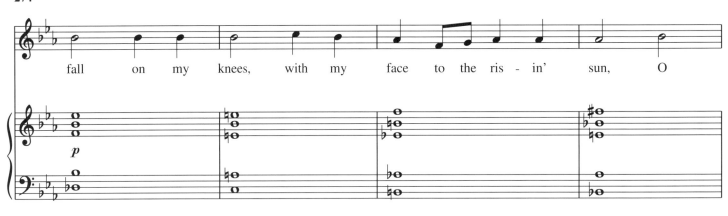

fall on my knees, with my face to the ris - in' sun, O

Lord, have mer - cy on me.

Let us praise God to -

geth - er on our knees, Let us praise God to -

(either R.H. or L.H.)

for Gayletha

Now Thank We All Our God

Martin Rinckart, c. 1636
translated by Catherine Winkworth, 1858

"Nun danket alle Gott"
melody by Johann Crüger, 1648
altered by Felix Mendelssohn, 1840
arranged by Richard Walters

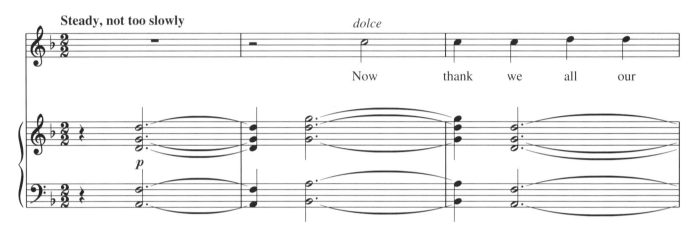

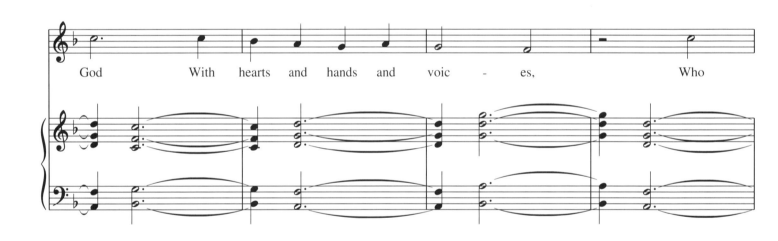

Copyright © 1993 by HAL LEONARD CORPORATION
International Copyright Secured   All Rights Reserved

Who, from our moth-er's arms Hath blessed us on our way With count-less gifts of love, And still is ours to-day.

O may this boun-teous God Through all our life be

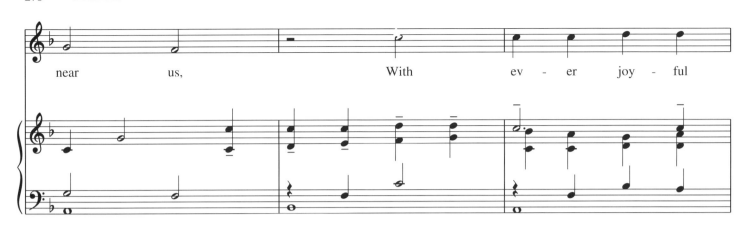

near us, With ev - er joy - ful

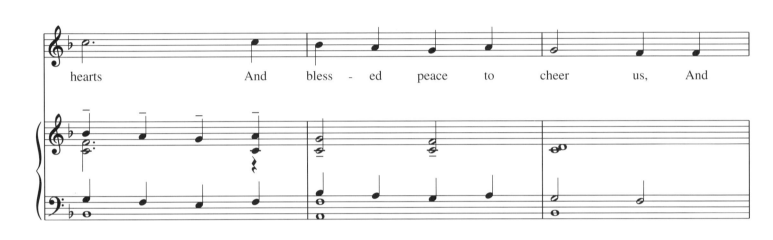

hearts And bless - ed peace to cheer us, And

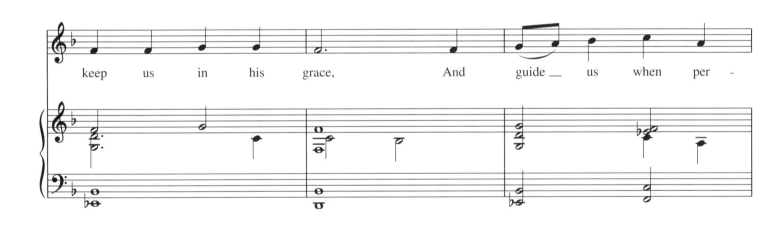

keep us in his grace, And guide __ us when per -

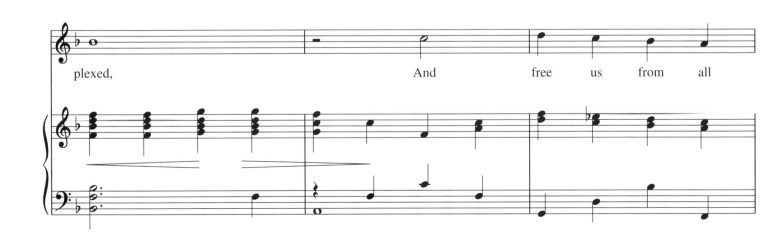

plexed, And free us from all

Son, and him who reigns with them in high-est heav-en,

The one e-ter-nal God, Whom

earth and heav'n a-dore

More Broadly to the End

For

thus it was, is now, And shall be ev-er more.

for Betsy and Harvey

O for a Thousand Tongues to Sing

Charles Wesley, 1739 (later altered)

Carl G. Gläser, 1784-1839
Mason's *Modern Psalmody,* 1839
arranged by Richard Walters

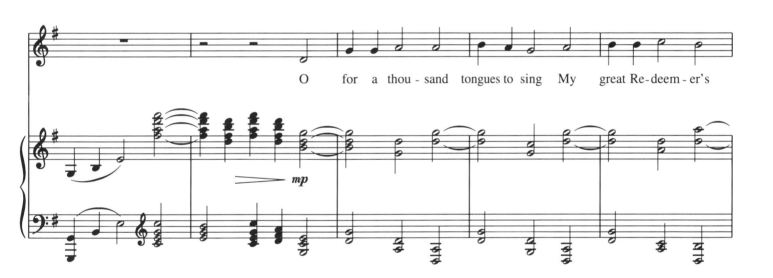

O for a thou-sand tongues to sing My great Re-deem-er's

praise, The glo-ries of my God and King, The __ tri-umphs of his grace.

Copyright © 1993 by HAL LEONARD CORPORATION
International Copyright Secured   All Rights Reserved

My gra-cious Mas - ter and my God, As - sist me to pro - claim, To spread thru all the earth a-broad The __ hon-ors of thy name.

A little slower

To God all glo - ry, praise and love Be now and ev - er

giv'n _____ By saints be - low

and saints a - bove The

church in earth and heav'n. _____

for Ida

Praise to the Lord, the Almighty

after Psalm 103
Joachim Neander, 1680
translated by Catherine Winkworth and others

"Lobe den Herren"
Ernewerten Gesangbuch, Stralsund, 1665
arranged by Richard Walters

Brightly, in 1

Praise to the Lord, the Al - might - y, the

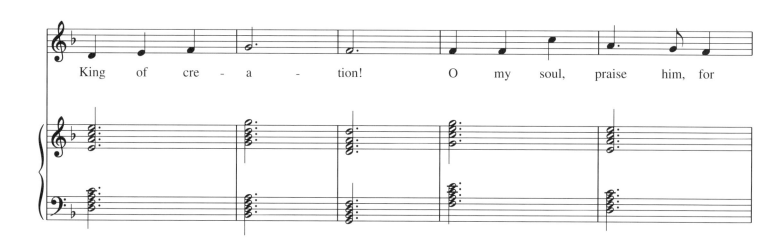

King of cre - a - tion! O my soul, praise him, for

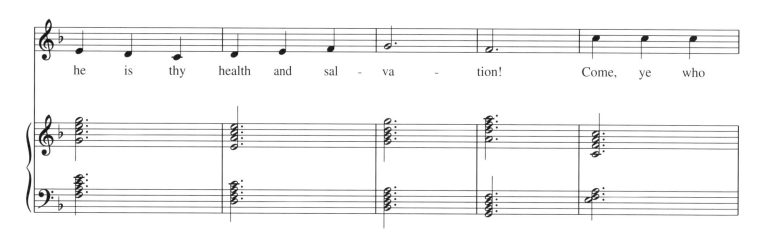

he is thy health and sal - va - tion! Come, ye who

Copyright © 1993 by HAL LEONARD CORPORATION
International Copyright Secured   All Rights Reserved

Shel - ters thee un - der his wings, yea, so gent - ly sus -

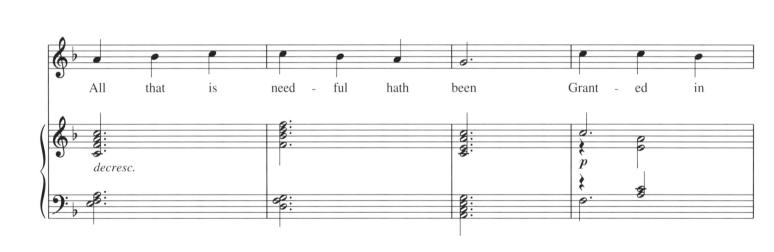

tain - eth! Hast thous not seen

All that is need - ful hath been Grant - ed in

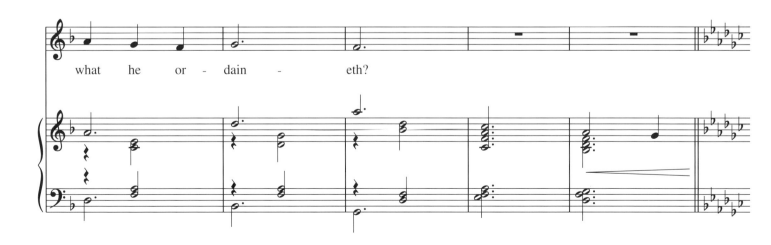

what he or - dain - eth?

do, He who with love doth be - friend thee.

Praise to the Lord! O let all that is in me a - dore him!

All that hath life and breath, come now with

for Reed

This Is My Father's World

Maltbie D. Babcock, 1901

traditional English melody
first adapted by Franklin L. Sheppard, 1915
arranged by Richard Walters

Copyright © 1993 by HAL LEONARD CORPORATION
International Copyright Secured   All Rights Reserved

This is my Fa-ther's world; I ___
rest me in the thought of rocks and trees, of ___
skies and seas; His hand ___ the won-ders ___ wrought.
This ___ is my Fa-ther's

speaks to me ev'ry-where.

A little slower

poco rit.

This is my Fa-ther's world; Oh,

let me ne'er for-get That though the wrong seems oft so strong, God

is the ru-ler yet. This is my Fa-ther's world, Why

should my heart be sad? The Lord is King, __ Let the heav - ens ring; __ God reigns, let the earth be glad. __

for Carol and Anne

We Are Climbing Jacob's Ladder

African-American Spiritual
Arranged by Richard Walters

Copyright © 2001 by HAL LEONARD CORPORATION
International Copyright Secured   All Rights Reserved

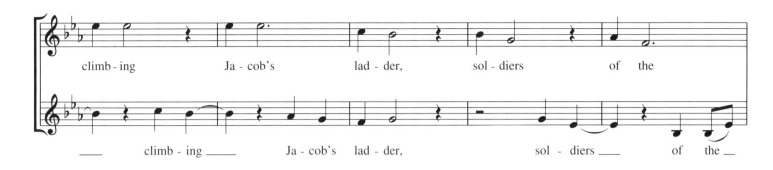

climb - ing Ja - cob's lad - der, sol - diers of the

___ climb - ing ____ Ja - cob's lad - der, sol - diers ___ of the ___

cross.

cross.

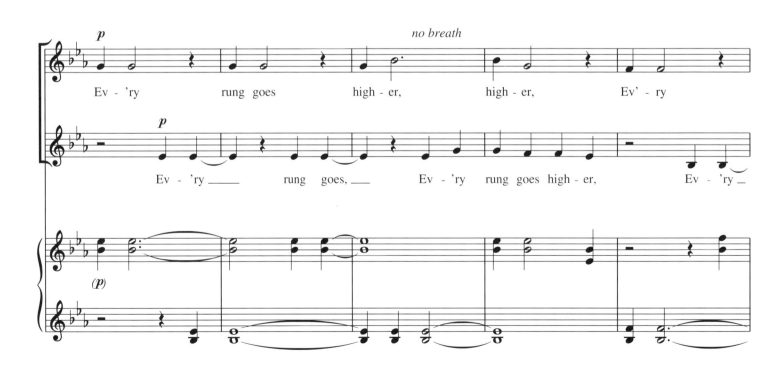

no breath

Ev - 'ry rung goes high - er, high - er, Ev' - ry

Ev - 'ry ____ rung goes, ___ Ev - 'ry rung goes high - er, Ev - 'ry ___

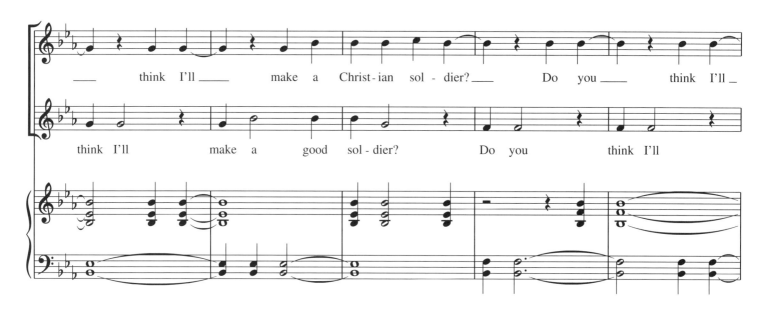

think I'll ___ make a Christ-ian sol-dier? ___ Do you ___ think I'll ___

think I'll make a good sol-dier? Do you think I'll

___ make a Christ-ian sol-dier? ___ Do you ___ think I'll ___ make a

make a good sol-dier? Do you think I'll make a good

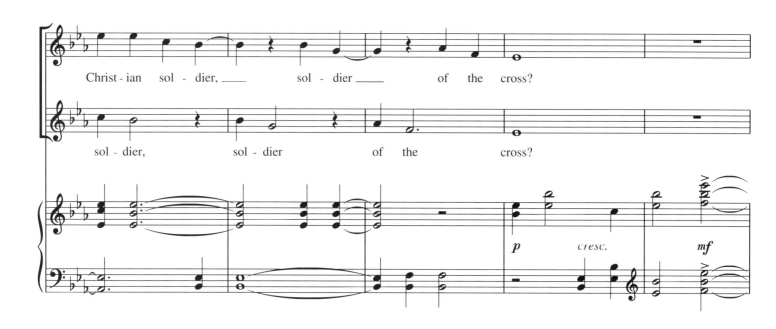

Christ-ian sol-dier, ___ sol-dier ___ of the cross?

sol-dier, sol-dier of the cross?

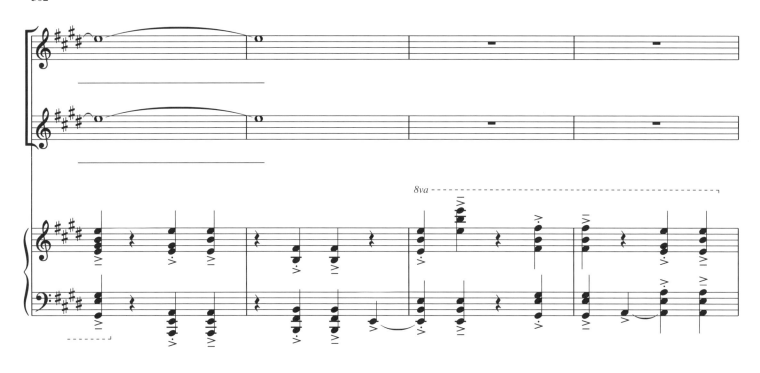

A Little Slower

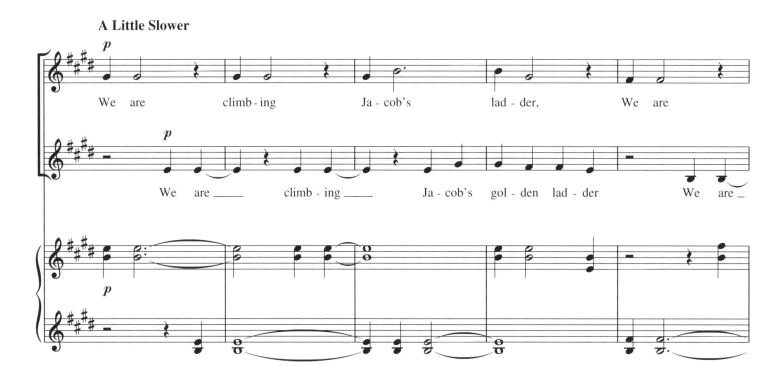

We are climb-ing Ja-cob's lad-der, We are

We are climb-ing Ja-cob's gol-den lad-der We are

for Paul and Lou

Wondrous Love

American Folk Hymn
arranged by Richard Walters

Copyright © 1992 by HAL LEONARD CORPORATION
International Copyright Secured   All Rights Reserved

bliss To bear the dread - ful curse for my

soul, for my soul, To bear the dread - ful curse for my

soul.

mp

lay a - side His crown for my soul, for my soul, He

soul, _____ O my

lay a - side His crown for my soul.

soul. _____

legato

mp

mp

High Voice:

What won-drous love is this, O my soul, O my

Medium Voice:

What won-drous love is

soul, What won-drous love is this, O my

this, O my soul O my soul, What

Slow, steady (♩. = ♩)

for my soul, for my soul, for my

for my soul, for my soul,

pp

soul, for my soul.

for my soul, for my soul.

mp

decresc. *poco rit.* *pp*